Rob Gronkowski

By K.C. Kelley

Consultant: Craig Ellenport,
Former Senior Editor, NFL.com

BEARPORT
PUBLISHING

New York, New York

Credits

Cover and Title Page: AP Photo/Evan Vucci; 4, © Kevin Dietsch/UPI/Newscom; 5, © EPA/Erik S. Lesser/Newscom; 6, © EPA/Erik S. Lesser/Newscom; 7, © Chris Coduto/Icon Sportswire 317/Newscom; 9, © Byron Purvis/AdMedia/Newscom; 10, © Peter Aiken/Cal Sport Media/Newscom; 11, © Mike Lynaugh/Amherst Bee; 12, © Bryan Smith/ZUMA Press/Newscom; 13, © Kevin P. Casey/Icon SMI 266/Newscom; 14, © AP Photo/Michael Dwyer; 15, © Aaron Souzzi/ZUMA Press/Newscom; 16, © Derrick Salters/WENN.com/Newscom; 17, © AP Photo/Steven Senne; 18, © EPA/Matt Campbell/Newscom; 19, © Joe Robbins; 20, © Eric Canha/CSM; 21, © Kevin Dietsch/UPI/Newscom; 22, © Anthony Nesmith/CSM/Newscom.

Publisher: Kenn Goin
Editor: Jessica Rudolph
Creative Director: Spencer Brinker
Photo Researcher: Shoreline Publishing Group LLC
Layout Design: Patty Kelley

Library of Congress Cataloging-in-Publication Data in process at time of publication (2016)
Library of Congress Control Nymber: 2015039373
ISBN-13: 978-1-943553-39-6

For more information, write to Bearport Publishing Company, Inc., 45 West 21st Street, Suite 3B, New York, New York 10010. Printed in the United States of America.

10 9 8 7 6 5 4 3 2 1

Contents

Time to Shine

On February 1, 2015, Rob Gronkowski had his eye on every football player's dream—an **NFL** championship. Rob and the New England Patriots were playing the Seattle Seahawks in **Super Bowl** XLIX (49). With less than a minute left in the first half, the two teams were tied 7–7. As the Patriots' star **tight end**, it was Rob's time to shine.

The Patriots run onto the field before the start of Super Bowl XLIX (49).

Rob is known to fans and teammates by his nickname, Gronk.

Gronk (#87) makes a catch in the first quarter of the Super Bowl as a Seahawks player tries to tackle him.

Champions!

Patriots **quarterback** Tom Brady went back to pass as Gronk sped down the field. Brady threw the ball high and far. Gronk caught it in the **end zone** for the **touchdown** and spiked the ball in celebration!

When the game was over, the Patriots had won 28–24. Gronk had the biggest smile in the stadium. Nothing felt better than winning a Super Bowl!

Gronk (#87) and Brady head to the bench after the touchdown.

The Patriots have played in eight Super Bowls. They're tied with the Dallas Cowboys and Pittsburgh Steelers for the most Super Bowl games ever played.

Gronk catches Brady's 22-yard (20 m) pass for a key touchdown during Super Bowl XLIX (49).

Growing Up Gronk

Gronk was born on May 14, 1989, in Amherst, New York. He grew up with four energetic brothers. In good weather, the boys played football, baseball, and basketball outdoors. Football was always Gronk's favorite sport. In bad weather, the boys played sports in the basement of their home. "It was a blast!" said Gronk.

Gronk is the second youngest of his brothers, but he grew up to be the biggest—6 feet 6 inches (2 m) and 265 pounds (120 kg).

The Gronkowskis at the 2015 ESPY Awards, an award show for athletes: (from left to right) father Gordon and brothers Dan, Gordie Jr., Rob, and Glenn

In high school, Gronk was a star on the football team. He usually played tight end but sometimes played on **defense**. Gronk could jump high to make incredible catches, and his strength made him very hard to tackle. As a senior, he was named an **All-American**. That meant Gronk was one of the best high school tight ends in the country!

Dan Gronkowski playing for the Denver Broncos

Gronk's brothers are also great at sports. Dan and Chris played on several NFL teams. Gordie Jr. played minor league baseball, and Glenn plays college football.

Gronk celebrates after scoring a touchdown for his high school football team, the Spartans.

College Days

In 2007, Gronk went to the University of Arizona. In his first season on the football team, he set a school record for tight ends. He **averaged** 18.8 yards (17.2 m) every time he caught a pass! In his second season, he caught more touchdowns than any other tight end in the school's history.

Gronk missed the following season because of a back injury. However, he worked hard to get better. In 2010, the New England Patriots chose him in the NFL **Draft**. Gronk had made it to the pros!

Gronk poses for a picture just before the 2010 NFL Draft in New York City.

Gronk playing for the University of Arizona Wildcats

Gronk was named to the All-Pac-10 team, which is similar to an all-star team. The Pac-10 is a group of colleges in the western United States whose sports teams play each other. It has since become the Pac-12.

13

A Record Start

Gronk started his **rookie** season with the Patriots in 2010. He was now playing with one of the greatest quarterbacks in history—Tom Brady. Brady believed in Gronk's abilities and helped him become a better receiver. "If Tom Brady believes I can do it, then I believe," Gronk said. In his first season, Gronk caught 10 touchdown passes. In 2011, he set an NFL record for tight ends with 17 touchdown catches!

Tom Brady (#12) talks with Gronk during a practice.

In Gronk's second season in the NFL, New England made it to Super Bowl XLVI (46). The Patriots lost to the New York Giants 21–17.

Gronk (#87) is tackled after he makes a catch in Super Bowl XLVI (46).

Unfortunately, Gronk's next two seasons were disappointing. In 2012, he broke his left arm when he was tackled. An **operation** was needed to fix an **infection** in the arm. In 2013, Gronk needed two more operations to fix injuries to his back and right knee. He had to take time off to get better. Gronk missed playing the game he loved.

Gronk's dad, Gordon, has always supported his son during tough times.

When Gronk hurt his right knee during a game in 2013, he was carried to the locker room for medical treatment.

After Gronk injured his knee, his father visited him in the locker room and held his hand. Gronk asked him, "Am I going to play again?" Gordon assured his son that he would return to the field.

Working Hard

Fortunately, no one works harder than Gronk. He was soon back in the gym, lifting weights and running. He was determined to play football again.

Gronk's hard work paid off. He made it back to the field for the 2014 season. He had a great year, catching 12 touchdowns. Best of all, the Patriots made it to the Super Bowl!

After he scores, Gronk often likes to spike the football into the ground to celebrate.

Gronk's enthusiasm and love for the game make him a fan favorite.

Gronk was the first NFL tight end to catch at least ten touchdowns in four different seasons.

A Great Comeback

During Super Bowl XLIX (49), Gronk made 6 catches for 68 yards (62.2 m). His touchdown catch was a key play. After coming back from all his injuries, Gronk was grateful that he could help lead his team to victory.

Patriots fans have stuck by Gronk through all his ups and downs, and he appreciates the support. He can't wait to make his fans proud for many more years to come!

During a parade to celebrate the Patriots' Super Bowl win, Gronk was all smiles for the fans.

Gronk (left) celebrates
with Tom Brady after
winning the Super Bowl.

WE ARE ALL PATRIOTS

In 2015, Gronk wrote
a book about his life and
career. It's called *It's
Good to Be Gronk*.

Gronk's Life and Career

★ **May 14, 1989** — Gronk is born in Amherst, New York.

★ **2007** — In his senior year of high school, Gronk is named an All-American.

★ **2007** — Gronk plays his first season with the University of Arizona.

★ **2010** — Gronk is drafted by the New England Patriots.

★ **2010** — As an NFL rookie, Gronk catches ten touchdown passes.

★ **2011** — With 17 touchdown catches, Gronk sets a single-season record for tight ends.

★ **2012** — The Patriots lose Super Bowl XLVI (46) to the New York Giants.

★ **2013** — Because of injuries to his arm, back, and knee, Gronk has several surgeries.

★ **2014** — Gronk recovers from his injuries and catches 12 touchdowns in the 2014 season.

★ **2015** — The Patriots win Super Bowl XLIX (49) over the Seattle Seahawks.

Glossary

All-American (awl-uh-MERR-uh-kuhn) a high school or college athlete who is named one of the best at his position in the entire country

averaged (AV-ur-ijd) had about the same amount over a series of events

defense (DEE-fenss) the part of a football team that tries to stop the other team from scoring

draft (DRAFT) an annual event during which NFL teams choose college players

end zone (END ZOHN) the area at either end of a football field where touchdowns are scored

infection (in-FEK-shuhn) an illness caused by germs

NFL (EN-EFF-ELL) letters standing for the National Football League, which includes 32 teams

operation (op-uh-RAY-shuhn) a procedure performed by a doctor to restore health or repair damage to a body

Pac-10 (PAK-TEN) a group of 10 (now 12) college football teams in the western United States that play against each other

quarterback (KWOR-tur-bak) a key player on offense for a football team who makes passes and hands the ball to teammates

rookie (RUK-ee) a player in his or her first season of a pro sport

Super Bowl (SOO-pur BOHL) the game played each year to determine the champion of the NFL

tight end (TYTE END) a player on the offense who catches passes and blocks for other players

touchdown (TUTCH-doun) a football scoring play worth six points that happens when a team gets the ball into the end zone

Index

Bibliography

Official Site of the New England Patriots: www.patriots.com

Official Site of the NFL: www.nfl.com

Read More

Frisch, Aaron. *New England Patriots (Super Bowl Champions).* Mankato, MN: Creative Education (2011).

Sandler, Michael. *Pro Football's Dream Teams (Fooball-O-Rama).* New York: Bearport (2011).

Whiting, Jim. *The Story of the New England Patriots (NFL Today).* Mankato, MN: Creative Education (2014).

Learn More Online

To learn more about Rob Gronkowski, visit
www.bearportpublishing.com/FootballStarsUpClose